Peter Oswald

ODYSSEUS

based on Homer's Iliad and Odyssey

OBERON BOOKS
LONDON

First published in 1999 by Oberon Books Ltd
(incorporating Absolute Classics)
521 Caledonian Road, London N7 9RH
Tel: 020 7607 3637 / Fax: 020 7607 3629
e-mail: oberon.books@btinternet.com

A catalogue record for this book is available from the
British Library.

ISBN: 1 84002 138 1

Cover design: Andrzej Klimowski

Typography: Richard Doust

Author photograph: John Timbers

Printed in Great Britain by MPG Books Ltd, Bodmin

Characters

ODYSSEUS

PENELOPE
his wife

TELEMACHOS
their son

ATHENE
a goddess

ANTINOOS
a suitor to Penelope

EUMAIOS
a swineherd

THEOKLYMENOS
a prophet

EURYKLEIA
nurse of Odysseus

IROS
a beggar

CHORUS
a ghost

Odysseus was first produced, as *The Odyssey*, at Chipping Norton Theatre on 20 September 1999, with the following cast:

ODYSSEUS, Leo Wringer

PENELOPE, Candida Gubbins

TELEMACHOS/IROS, Robert Bladen

ATHENE/EURYKLEIA, Vanessa Earl

ANTINOOS, Neil Cornrich

EUMAIOS, Stephen Gurney

CHORUS, Members of the company

Director: Martin Wylde

Designer: Roger Butlin

The production transferred to the Gate Theatre, London, on 20 October 1999.

The play takes place on the island of Ithaka.

Scene 1

The palace of ODYSSEUS. Enter PENELOPE.

PENELOPE: One day my husband, King Odysseus,
    Sailed with Achilles under Agamemnon
    For Troy. Then twenty waiting years uplifted
    Our son. And now returning Agamemnon
    Has been cut down at supper by the lover
    Of his inhuman wife, and half our fighters
    Are scattered over ocean. Thieves and cowards
    Reign in their kingdoms. For the last three years
    A band of suitors, with their retinues,
    Has feasted in the palace of Odysseus,
    Demanding me. I am too weak to stop them,
    And now my son Telemachos has left me
    To find his father, and they plan to kill him
    When he returns. Pallas Athene, help me!

    Enter ANTINOOS.

ANTINOOS: Penelope.

PENELOPE: Antinoos, my friend.
    You are the grandest of the noblemen
    Who occupy my husband's palace, feeding
    On his possessions, asking for my hand,
    In the belief that he will not come home,
    But has been swallowed by a sea-monster
    Or sold in Egypt to the Pharaoh's mistress,
    And if I wish to speak to all of you
    At once, then it is you that I should speak to.

ANTINOOS: What do you wish to say, why have you
                      called me
    So early in the morning, my good lady?
    Have you decided to relent? Your mind
    Is wider than the wander of a seagull;
    When we arrived, you seemed an easy sea,

And it was rumoured that the other side
Was no more than a wind-blown year away,
Yet here we are still pulling at the oars.

PENELOPE: I am still married.

ANTINOOS: After twenty years
We can presume that you have lost your husband.
Embrace the pain. Recover. Start again.
New life is rising, pressing in on you
At every point. You can no more refuse it
Than the wide ocean can refuse its rivers.

PENELOPE: If I must choose, and I suppose I must,
To save this house, so that my son can have it –
Who shall it be? Antinoos, advise me!

ANTINOOS: Terrible question! Who could I commend?
Antinoos is not the worst of us –
Foremost in fear and weakness though he is.

PENELOPE: So I believe.

ANTINOOS: Go on, Penelope.
Now you can tell me what you think of me.

PENELOPE: And thus Aegistheus gave himself away;
Clytaemnestra melted in his fire
And they collapsed together to the floor,
To talk about the death of Agamemnon
In his own palace –

ANTINOOS: Why am I Aegistheus?
There is no murder necessary here,
The sea has done it.

PENELOPE: What about my son?

ANTINOOS is silenced.

Antinoos, the best of my admirers!
If there is really none as good as you,

6

And I must choose one, I am in deep water.
A hundred men who love me in my house –
The best of Ithaka itself, Zakynthos,
Doulichion and Same – Agelaos,
Who is not all that stupid, wise Leodes,
Peisandros, furious Ktessipos,
Bitter Eurydamas, Eurymochos
The swift, and generous Amphinomos –
The finest men alive no doubt, and yet
Not one is better than Odysseus dead,
If I am looking at the best of them!
Your friends are waiting in a ship to murder
My son.

ANTINOOS: These things will happen. We are many,
And you have kept us waiting at your table
For three years, face to face with one another,
Increasing one another's heat like mirrors!
For a long time you tricked us. Like Odysseus
Your mind is deep, although the sea is deeper.
Weaving a shroud, you said, for old Laertes –
When it was finished you would choose a husband,
But every night your nimble hands unravelled
What you had done by daylight, and the labour
Was everlasting, and Laertes, clearly,
Immortal, till we heard about your nightwork,
And how each dawn you mocked our expectation
And all our lives kept waiting to be happy!

PENELOPE: Will you prevent the murder of my son?

ANTINOOS: I was against it, and the man who does it
Will, on that instant, find unending death
On my spear's point, I swear to you by Hades
Where I will send him clutching at his deathwound.
I will announce this to the rest of us.
Your son must not be harmed. But if wide heaven
And Zeus who rules Olympus have decided
Against him, he is dead. If they desire

To give me you, you will be mine in time,
If not, then scatter to the seven winds
My body and the body of your son,
Since all my waiting will have come to nothing!
We understand each other then. I save
Your son from being murdered. In return
You will choose one of us today.

PENELOPE: Today?
Give me at least a night to dream about it.

ANTINOOS: Tomorrow then.

PENELOPE: Tomorrow it shall be.

ANTINOOS: You see, all things that live must love, or die.

Exit PENELOPE.

Odysseus, if you are alive
Somewhere, at home you have just died.

Exit.

Scene 2

The farm of EUMAIOS. Enter EUMAIOS.

EUMAIOS: Now what's this noble shape approaching,
                                        looming
Out of the dawn? A rearing bear, a dryad,
Or something bad? Oh Zeus, Telemachos!

Enter TELEMACHOS. EUMAIOS embraces him.

TELEMACHOS: Eumaios, father!

EUMAIOS: Have you seen your father?

TELEMACHOS: Certainly not.

EUMAIOS: But he is here in you,
Telemachos, sweet light! Oh thank you heaven.
Oh let me feast my heart with looking at you.

8

I thought I'd never see your face again
When you took ship for Pylos. And your mother
Gave up completely.

TELEMACHOS: Do you mean, Eumaios,
That she has married?

EUMAIOS: No, I only meant
That she gave up on you. But tell me quickly,
What have you seen? Why did you leave?

TELEMACHOS: Athene.
She came to me, and told me to abandon
My childhood, and to speak against the suitors
In the assembly. So I did. I told them
That they are dead. They cursed me to my face,
And I walked out and with a few companions
Sailed to the mainland and King Menelaos,
And we met Helen, and she prophesied
That we will see Odysseus very shortly,
But I am not sure.

EUMAIOS: I am not sure either.
I would not trust that woman very far;
No, it all rests upon Penelope,
My faith in women – if she falls, well then,
To blazes with the bloody lot of them.

TELEMACHOS: When Menelaos talked about the war,
We wept, and Helen brought us cups of wine
In which she had infused a preparation
That made us dance and sing. If we had seen
Our mothers torn by dogs before our eyes,
We would have laughed, so strong was that concoction.

He spits.

Well we sailed home, and on the way the suitors
Were waiting in a ship to cut my head off,
But we slipped by them. So you see, Eumaios.

9

EUMAIOS: They tried to kill you but you got away!

TELEMACHOS: But I thought hard, and thought it
                                    would be best
     Not to go straight home, but to see you first,
     You are my father.

EUMAIOS: I am not Odysseus.

TELEMACHOS: Where is he then? The sea is everything.
     From this high hill look down in all directions;
     No father from horizon to horizon.

EUMAIOS: So you have been to Pylos, and the sea
     Is a bit bigger than you thought it was.
     But you went looking for Odysseus
     Because Athene told you to, and Helen
     Told you in Sparta that he is returning.

TELEMACHOS: There are these voices. One
                                    a mortal woman
     Whose lust destroyed ten thousand men, the other
     A flash, a star beyond our understanding.
     No, when I think of the unending ocean,
     I do not think that you will see that man
     Alive again. And I have never seen him.
     You are my father.

EUMAIOS: I am not Odysseus.
     That much I know for sure. Oh King and Captain,
     I think the sea has carried you away,
     Mostly because, whatever Helen says,
     I am inclined to think the opposite.
     And in the palace of Odysseus
     Nothing will stop the suitors from their slaughter,
     Making your mother's maids their whores, demanding
     Your mother as the best of them, consuming
     Your father's wealth, so as to leave you nothing,
     Murdering strangers, as the god forbade us.

TELEMACHOS: So you have given up all hope of him;
    Then you must think that I should give my mother
    In marriage to the foremost of the suitors,
    Since I am now a man and not a boy,
    And while I keep her in my house, those men
    Will carry on consuming my possessions.

EUMAIOS: Marry your mother to Antinoos?
    That would be very trivial advice.

TELEMACHOS: What shall I do then?

EUMAIOS: Scream and stamp your feet,
    Shout at the ground to give you back Odysseus!

TELEMACHOS: Dig for Odysseus! Heap up worlds
                          of earth!

EUMAIOS: Calm down! The man has vanished –
                        be resigned –

TELEMACHOS: Marry my mother to Antinoos –

EUMAIOS: No! But don't not. Oh! See – I'm
                       not Odysseus!
    I am Eumaios, all the time. Odysseus
    Was I suppose, above all things, surprising.
    Like when he left – that was precisely like him –
    Well you were there.

TELEMACHOS: But I was just a baby –

EUMAIOS: Of course you know he didn't want to go.
    Nor did Achilles. It was pitiful;
    Achilles hid by putting on a dress,
    Odysseus, he pretended to be mad,
    And took an ox and hitched it to a plough
    And cut a furrow right along the sand,
    And then another, winking down the line
    To keep it straighter than a square. The gulls
    Looking for worms, as if it was a field,

Were absolutely fooled, and boys and girls
Cackled like magpies up and down the shore,
Scattering bags of pebbles in the sea;
Then Agamemnon, who had come for him,
To take him with his army far away
For a long time – but no one knew how long –
Picked up that ploughman's son and laid him down
Bang in the path of the approaching share
And the big ox. And there you lay, and smiled,
And poor Odysseus turned the beast aside
And picked you up, and, crying like a child,
Said, 'You have made me give myself away,
To save you I must sail away to Troy,
And never hold you in my arms again.
You will be far too old when I return,
If I return. Goodbye, my little boy.'

TELEMACHOS: That was the last I ever saw of him.

EUMAIOS: That was the end of peace in Ithaka.
Now we have murder in its place, a gang
Instead of one, each wanting everything,
And pouring blood and filth into the ground
Where it won't go unnoticed, but will nourish
A crop of swords! Bad luck will come to them,
Whether or not Odysseus comes back home!

TELEMACHOS: This is my introduction to it all,
I step across the threshold of the world
Straight into exile – not to run away,
But to be hunted in my father's country!

EUMAIOS: When you should hunt them!

TELEMACHOS: He has not returned.
You are my father, since I need advice,
Friendship, protection. Small things can be done.
Well I will stay here for the night at least;
Then I would have you go down to the city

To tell my mother that I am alive,
And not to marry yet – but then, who knows,
Ithaka is a leaky raft to me,
And the sea rising. Let me go inside.

Exeunt.

Scene 3

The shore of Ithaka. ODYSSEUS lies asleep. Enter ATHENE.

ATHENE: It is Athene! From the ear
Of Zeus, already armed, I sprang.
To burn down Troy I fought my father,
That was the price for stolen Helen.
Now for Penelope the wise
I have returned this shipwrecked man.
Oh I have held them in my hands,
Apart, so long, in suffering,
To keep the price of love increasing;
That is my lonely work, my passion.
Because your mind is like my own,
My friend, my child, my fascination!
Thanks to Athene you are home.
The good Phaiakians brought you here,
You fell asleep on board, they lifted
The King, still sleeping like a baby,
And set him down in his own country.
Now the sun climbs into his eyes –
But he must still depend on me!

ATHENE stands ODYSSEUS on his feet and spins him round, then goes to the side and looks on. ODYSSEUS wakes up, and looks around, confused and aghast.

ODYSSEUS: O Leucothoe, on the changing sea,
Dangerous-white – I gave you back your veil
When I was rescued by the river's mouth.

Not looking back, I let it go, as promised,
Downwind – so seagull, why do you accuse me?
No, not accusing, dipping in the green
Its head and wide wings, shrugging off some stain
Or failure. I should be in Ithaka.
Why is my heart not dancing? Everything
Should be as well known as the sun and moon,
There should be rocks I recognise, and dunes
That clap me on the shoulder like a dad.
Even the seaweed ought to speak to me
In Ithaka – but nothing's happening.

CHORUS: The goddess has abandoned him
And he is in the world alone!
Fall to your knees and count the sand!

ODYSSEUS: Dead friend, are you still standing on
my shadow?
Who are you, Aias, Meges, Elpenor?
Is there no room in Hades, must you dog me,
Giving me bad advice and frightening me?
Well you and I must work this out together.
Either this shoreline is not Ithaka's,
Or simply I am not Odysseus,
And even if I saw my wife and son,
My heart would crouch down like a fox inside me,
Waiting to see what happened next. Athene,
Why did you save me from the bitter sea?
If I am not myself, if I am No one,
Think of it – then there is no Ithaka,
No end at all to all my journeying!

ATHENE: (*Aside.*)
Although my heart goes out to him,
I have to leave him for awhile,
To weigh on terrifying scales
His mortal soul against my own.
How else can there be talk between us?

ODYSSEUS: That was a gulf I skipped across unwinged,
 But I have crossed with this consideration:
 Clearly my friends the brave Phaiakians,
 Those more-than-god-like honourable men,
 Who promised to convey me with all speed
 To Ithaka, are like the rest of us,
 Capable of deception – should I say,
 A load of filthy Thracians, dogs, pigs, thieves,
 Gibbering witches looking for a profit
 Out of a poor man. They have put me down
 At the pathetic edge of some thin kingdom
 Peopled by goats! And all my sufferings
 Have got me nowhere. But to trust an air
 Of honour, oh you girl, Odysseus –
 Counsellor, hero, you have sold yourself.
 Ah but their streets, their mile-high palaces,
 Tiled speeches, flying-buttressed promises –
 Winds in a weak bag. Strong man, start again,
 Wiser, world-wide, not beaten but worn down
 Into the shape of a smooth skimming-stone.

ATHENE: (*Aside.*)
 Think hard, let nothing slip your mind,
 It is the passion of a goddess
 That pours upon you, not her pity.

ODYSSEUS: And I embarked from Troy that happy day
 With twelve ships of companions. Where are they?
 Eurybates, Eurylochos the rebel,
 Antiphos and my friend Perimides,
 Poor Elpenor – I saved them from the war,
 But on the way home lost the lot of them.

CHORUS: We steered our ships into a bay,
 Ringed with black cliffs. You stayed outside.
 And giants rained down rocks upon us –
 Men without hands, trying to swim –
 And we cried out to our captain and our king!

ODYSSEUS: The shark, the mermaid and the squid
    Feed on my friends and are well-fed;
    The son, the mother and the bride
    Sleep in a bed whose dreams are void.

    ODYSSEUS throws himself to the ground and lies still.
    ATHENE steps into the centre.

ATHENE: Now I must pick him up again,
    Since he is pressed against the face
    Of his mortality; it's time
    To entertain him with his destiny.
    So I shall be a shepherd boy
    Happening by, and helpfully
    Explain his whereabouts. And he,
    Oh he will lie to me. My friend,
    What are you doing weeping on the sand,
    Crawling about as if you were a crab
    Whose shell a child had prised off for a game,
    Beating the peaceful seashells with your hands
    And hurling rocks into the heaped-up foam?
    Have you been shipwrecked?

ODYSSEUS: Tell me where I am.

ATHENE: Funny old fellow! You were born this morning
    If you have never heard of – well this country
    Is not unknown. It is a rugged island,
    Not wide or good for racing horses in,
    But it produces barley, wheat and wine,
    And there is always plenty of sweet rain
    To keep them coming. There are goats and cattle,
    Excellent springs and wells, all kinds of timber;
    Its name is known as far away as Troy,
    And Troy, they say, is very far away;
    I think you must have heard of Ithaka.

ODYSSEUS: Thank you. I have. When I was on the island
   Of Crete before I sailed to Troy, I heard it.
   I am an exile. I have killed a man,
   Orsilochos of Crete, the son of great
   Idomeneus, and the swiftest runner
   In that whole island. But the sprinter tried
   To take my share of what we took from Troy,
   Because I would not join his company
   To please his father, but instead desired
   To lead my own men. So, with one of them,
   I hid beside the road at night and struck him
   With the spear's bronze as he was heading homewards.
   There was a dark night spread across the sky,
   Which kept the deed unseen, and I went down
   And made a bargain with the proud Phoenicians
   To take me, for a share of spoil, to Pylos
   In a fast ship, or else to shining Elis,
   And they agreed, but, beaten by the wind,
   We had to shelter here. We piled, storm-haggard,
   Onto the sand, and slept. But while I dreamed,
   They woke and took their ship back home to Sidon.

ATHENE: (*As herself.*)
   You'll talk your way past death, my friend,
   You are so like myself! But are you blind?
   What can have happened to my flashing eyes?

ODYSSEUS: How can men know you, bright one, when
                                             you are
   At any time, in any place, whatever
   You want to be – I only know for certain
   When you are not there, which is all too often;
   You left me helpless in the bitter sea.
   Your love is strange, it is your trick to say
   That I am home, that this is Ithaka.
   You are so full of light, you wanted me
   To lie to you so you could laugh at me!

ATHENE: How can I ever let you go
　　When you will not let go of me,
　　Child of my heart! What fox could ever
　　Outskip your thinking, that will never
　　Stand still, not even in your homeland!
　　I only want you to be happy.
　　Oh child! How could you have imagined
　　That I could ever leave you dying
　　On the wide sea? I knew for certain
　　That you would find your way back home,
　　Alone, at last, without companions.
　　And see the truth of what I say!

ODYSSEUS: Then take me to Penelope.
　　Without your power I am nowhere.

ATHENE: Well you are somewhere if I love you.
　　Now look around at Ithaka!

ATHENE touches ODYSSEUS and his eyes are opened.

ODYSSEUS: This is the harbour that belongs to Phorkys,
　　The old man of the sea. The olive tree
　　Stands on its shadow by the Naiads' cave,
　　Full of their treasure. I can see the mountain
　　Neritos; and its shape proclaims this place
　　Ithaka – goddess, you have given this!

ATHENE: I sent Telemachos your son
　　To search for you, and be a man;
　　He has returned, and you will find him
　　Sheltering with your slave Eumaios.
　　It is my wish that with the blood
　　And entrails of ungracious men
　　Your palace shall be spattered soon.
　　And so I make you old to trick them,
　　But when the time comes, youth will spring!

She touches him and makes him old.

ODYSSEUS: The anger of the dead is nothing
    Next to your love when it returns.

Exeunt.

Scene 4

The farm of EUMAIOS. Enter TELEMACHOS.

TELEMACHOS: Go to the city and be killed, stay here,
    And wait to hear the news that she is married –
    Nothing and nothing are my choices now,
    This is the life that lies in front of me,
    Drifting and singing. So I sink, unseen.

He breaks down. Enter EUMAIOS.

EUMAIOS: Stand up, young man! Your home is in
                          the hands
    Of murderers, the kingdom of your father
    Is clouded over by their dark desires –
    But your decision to decline is wrong.
    Look how the sun, that has seen everything,
    Still gets up bright and early in the morning
    To fight the mists of madness. Now its eye
    Is set on noon. The worst thing that can happen
    To us is nothing, which will be our doing,
    So let's get going. Look at me, a slave,
    Whose life's a leaking sack of sand, achieving
    Nothing for him, encouraging a king's son!
    There's absolutely nothing to be done
    About these days, and we must start today.
    See to the stock, sit by a fire outside
    Where you can see the compensating sky,
    That's what I do. You dig into your dreams,
    And if you find your father in them, fine.

TELEMACHOS jumps up.

What have you seen, young man, a flaming Titan?

TELEMACHOS: Who is this stranger straining up
                                    the hill?
    Old fellow! Welcome to our native country!
    How did you get here? I have never seen
    Your face before among our stones and mountains.
    I do not think you walked to Ithaka.
    But you can tell us later who you are,
    And all your story. Come beside the fire,
    This man will bring you food and heap up branches
    For you to sit on. You have travelled far,
    If years are miles, and it would not be fair
    For your old bones to be your only chair.

Enter ODYSSEUS out of breath.

ODYSSEUS: May Zeus the father grant your
                                    heart's desires,
    For giving comfort to a wanderer.

TELEMACHOS: Not even Zeus can be of use to us,
    Believe me, sir. But that's another matter.
    As for the welcome we have given you,
    How could we treat you any other way?
    How would we dare, since guests and strangers are
    Sacred to Zeus almighty. There are men,
    Who do no honour to the god of strangers,
    But we are not like them, because misfortune
    Has touched us too, and blessed us with compassion.
    So take your ease. But we will use your wisdom,
    If you have wisdom. We were just complaining
    About the situation in this island;
    Our lord is never likely to return,
    And there are men who want to kill his son,
    Mad birds too strange to nest, who trick hard workers;
    They want his wealth. You see, you have arrived
    In an unpeaceful territory. Listen –
    Would you advise the honourable woman
    Who has for so long waited for this man,

  To take a villain from among the brigands
  Who weigh upon her with their one suggestion?

ODYSSEUS: Your lord is not dead. You must tell his lady
  Not to relent.

TELEMACHOS: Aha, a crazy man!
  Just what we need!

ODYSSEUS: If this is Ithaka,
  The lord you mention is Odysseus.
  He is not dead. I may have lost my mind,
  As old men do, but if I am alive
  So is Odysseus.

TELEMACHOS: How would that be proof?

EUMAIOS: Many have said so to Penelope,
  To get a small reward and see her cry.

ODYSSEUS: If King Odysseus does not come
            back home –
  Hack off my head, and kick it down this hill
  Up which I've lugged it. Do it anyway,
  It's not much good.

EUMAIOS: And how would Zeus reward me
  For that! I see that you are wise. Thank heaven
  You came to help us in our time of trouble!

TELEMACHOS: Tell us your crazy story, anyway.

ODYSSEUS: I was at Troy. I fought beside Odysseus.
  And I returned to Crete, which is my home.
  I am the son of Kastor, son of noble
  Hylakos; but I could not rest at ease.
  After one month I had to lead my men
  To Egypt and was captured on the plain
  Where the Aegyptos pours into the sea,
  But I was favoured by the King of Egypt,
  Until the lies of a Phoenician man

Led me aboard his vessel to be sold
In Libya; but on the open sea
Zeus struck his vessel with a thunderbolt,
And all the crew were washed away. But I,
Gripping the snapped keel, drifted for six days.
The tempest drove me to Thesprotia,
And where a river, speaking to the sea
Out of its clear throat, sweetens the salt water,
I crept out, crusted with a scurf of salt.

CHORUS: With thoughts that rush like stormclouds
dancing
Over the sea on stilts of lightning,
How easily you change your story.

ODYSSEUS: And in that place by luck the son of Pheidon,
The great King, found me, and he carried me
Back to his father's palace, and the King
Put me aboard a ship to take me home.

ATHENE: (*Aside.*)
Miracle of the mind! To find,
At the very edge of nothing,
Rising from the cliff like martins,
Fabrications, inspirations!

ODYSSEUS: But these Thesprotians, as I should
have known,
Had no intention of conveying me
To Crete, but stripped me, out of sight of land,
Bound me, and clothed me with this cloak of rags,
Meaning to sell me into slavery.
They left me in the ship at Ithaka,
Which they left anchored while they slept ashore,
And I escaped into the waves and swam
Through the black water full of stars that clustered
Around my fingers, to the land, whose shadows
Gathered me coldly. So I come alone,
Fatherless offspring of the childless ocean.

ATHENE: (*Aside.*)
  Some alterations of the names
  Change nothing of the suffering.

TELEMACHOS: Credible. Well said. Maybe even true.

EUMAIOS: You tell us that Odysseus is alive.
  How do you know? You fought with him at Troy,
  But Troy was burned to dust ten years ago.

ODYSSEUS: When I was in Thesprotia I was told
  That he had been their guest, your vanished lord,
  Not long before, but, full of thoughts, had gone
  To listen to the oak tree at Dodona
  Through which Zeus speaks, in order to discover
  Whether he should return to Ithaka
  After so long, in plain sight, or in secret.

TELEMACHOS: Old man, you have been wandering,
                                                I see,

  Among much talk of our predicament –
  There is much speculation in the islands,
  Clearly, rewards for stories. I have seen
  Truth in an old man, like a shining mountain,
  Nestor I mean, but you are not like him.
  To make my father walk across your tongue
  Out of your mind's weak dreams – abomination
  Beyond forgiveness! He will not return!
  And you have made him vile with your invention!

EUMAIOS: Telemachos, be patient with his dotage,
  It is not right to undermine old men,
  He is a stranger, and the god protects him,
  And if it happened and that man returned,
  Then you would bless this old man's revelations,
  Which are not something for a man to rage at.

TELEMACHOS: Eumaios, you are right and
                                      I am sorry.
  Old fool, forgive my mood. You may be mad,

23

But we can only join you in your madness,
Yield to your lie – or else dismiss my father,
Who is at present most alive in rumours.
I am his son, insane Telemachos.
Since we are all fools, you can stay with us,
And help us with our howling. So Eumaios,
Father, go down, and tell Penelope,
Starving for news, that I am safely home,
And then return to me and to this man,
And may the god befriend us.

EUMAIOS: I will tell her.

Exit EUMAIOS.

TELEMACHOS: Now I will fetch more wood.
                                        The fire is dying,
And there is not much courage in the sun.

Exit.

CHORUS: So now the son disdains the father
As if a ship disdained a harbour
In a high sea, and turned again
Into numb nothing and destruction.

ODYSSEUS: Listen to me, Athene! Shall I tell
My son, my heart's true harbour, who I am,
Or shall I carry on equivocating
My name? The darkness that exists between us
Drowns me. My tired imagination longs
To stop pretending, and to speak to him.

Re-enter TELEMACHOS with wood.

TELEMACHOS: Old man, you seem distracted.

ODYSSEUS: In my mind,
The people and the places I have seen
Will not lie down. They walk and talk. The wind

24

Still blows me backwards to the company
Of men now bones, and in their graves I dine.

TELEMACHOS: I will be mad before my hair is grey.
People go mad much younger nowadays.
My friend the swineherd is already mad.
He is as loyal to my father's cause
As I am – and my life depends on him.

Exit.

ODYSSEUS: I need you goddess! On the sea
When I was gasping like a baby
I did not need you more than now
I need my son to recognise me!

Enter ATHENE.

ATHENE: I will make you everything,
I will give you stars and moons,
I will kiss you in your dreams;
You must take your sword and cut
Out your heart and I will put
Songs of summer into it,
I will put you back together,
Chase the dead into the ground.
Just for a moment you will be
Just as you are, for him to see.
Beautiful man, be beautiful again.

She touches him and restores him, then exits.

*Re-enter TELEMACHOS, who drops the wood in amazement
and kneels, with his hands over his eyes.*

TELEMACHOS: I was mistaken! Oh forgive me then,
If I said anything against you, great one,
When I believed that you were just a man,
Whichever god you are, whose shape can change.

ODYSSEUS: Do not compare me with the gods, my son.

TELEMACHOS: Do not pretend to be Odysseus!

ODYSSEUS: You must believe that I am him. No other
Odysseus will return to you, believe me.

TELEMACHOS: You are a god who wants to see
me crying.

ODYSSEUS: Grey-eyed Athene gave me that disguise,
I have the wit to use it. It was she
Who chased away my death and brought me here
In order that the men who threaten you
Should not keep out your daylight anymore.

TELMACHOS and ODYSSEUS stand staring at each other.

ATHENE: (*Aside.*)
See how the world recycles water,
That falls as grey rain everywhere,
And rises to the eyes as tears
That seek the sea down cheeks and chins.
Oh there is so much water in the world,
All of it falling and reflecting,
Everything weeping in the arms
Of everything – the sun brought down
Into a puddle, and the moon
Undone by drips into a drain.

TELEMACHOS breaks down and they embrace.

ODYSSEUS: You see I am not mad.

TELEMACHOS: There are too many
Against us, father, waiting in the valley.

ODYSSEUS: But with Athene we are more than them.
We will go down into the valley now,
And you will take your mother by the hand,
But tell her nothing yet. And we must part

Before we reach the palace, not to enter
Together. Then we must begin pretending.
And they will curse me, even knock me down,
That is their way, and their self-condemnation.
You must not raise a hand to help me, mutter,
Or wipe away a tear. Ignore their fury,
These shoulders have endured worse storms, believe me.

ATHENE touches ODYSSEUS and makes him old again.

ATHENE: With this I blind the eyes
Of those about to die.
Enter your home again,
A sight to be despised.
If only men could see
How carefully disguised
Catastrophe creeps in!

Exit.

TELEMACHOS: I glimpsed you for a moment as
you were,
And now my eyes have made you old again.

ODYSSEUS: It is the goddess. I am still the same.

Exeunt.

Scene 5

PENELOPE downstairs in the palace with EUMAIOS.

PENELOPE: You tell me that Telemachos has come
Safely through ambush back to Ithaka,
And I am to rejoice and weep no more,
Although the men who planned his death are now
Not pigs but wolves, and all because my son,
Without consulting me, stood up to them,
Which roused the suitors, snorting, stamping, herd,
From a trough stupor to starvation fury.
My scale is lower than at any time

In the last twenty years, Telemachos
Has changed our politics to violence
By what he did, and only Zeus, or chance,
Preserved his life. My son cannot imagine
How carefully I keep the suitors hoping.

EUMAIOS: You make them yearn. And this is how
your son
Lives with regard to his beloved father.

PENELOPE: I know, I know, the possibility,
The how-it-could-be, drives you half-insane,
If you allow it. And my son is young
And thinks that he can change things with his hands,
Whereas the wider stream and drift of things
Cannot be altered. You can turn around
A boat, but not the ocean. Oh Eumaios,
Is he alright?

EUMAIOS: Your son is safe, my lady.
Not only safe, but braver than he was.

PENELOPE: I was afraid of that.

EUMAIOS: And his horizons
Are broadened.

PENELOPE: We will have to stretch to them.

EUMAIOS: He has met Helen.

PENELOPE: Well-connected man!

EUMAIOS: And Menelaos.

PENELOPE: Lots to learn from him.

EUMAIOS: The very ancient Nestor.

PENELOPE: Just in time!

EUMAIOS: He has survived the hatred of the suitors,
He was a boy but now he is a man.

Between these two conditions stood a door,
And at the door stood murder, axe in hand.
As dangerous as kicking snakes to pass,
But absolutely necessary, and
The gods exist to help us with these things.

PENELOPE: Yes, and the dream is very sweet, my friend,
And restless in the head, and who am I
To tell him to resist it! Every month
Some rumour of my husband reaches us,
Like the slow waves that rise far out to sea
And travel grandly to the shore to shatter,
And walking by the sea I sometimes wonder
If his heart beating in some deep sea cavern
Causes these rhythms pushing at my footprints.
My husband is the source of many stories,
That has not changed. But can we, with our hands,
Transform them into solid flesh and bone?
Are rumours like the living spirit wind
With which the god turned dust into a man?
I think that they have no such potency,
And so, since life refuses to be raised
Out of the sand and gravel of these times,
We must do likewise, and remain calm stone.

EUMAIOS: So you will marry one of them today,
Antinoos, or sweet Ktessipos?

PENELOPE: You may not like them much, Eumaios, but
Nor do you like providing them with suppers.
The choice is mine, to save my son's possessions
So that in time, he too can marry, choosing
The best of many, not necessity,
Which is a hard wife and at best unhappy.

EUMAIOS: Yes, but Odysseus –

PENELOPE: He is dead, Eumaios.

EUMAIOS: How do you know?

PENELOPE: He told me so himself.

EUMAIOS: What do you mean?

PENELOPE: He said that I should marry
If he did not return to Ithaka
Before his son became a man. That day
Is now upon us, since Telemachos
Has spoken out against the suitors; swineherd,
Give me a hope for my Odysseus
And I will stand like ice against these liars.

EUMAIOS: I would have said another man has come,
Who swears as if he feared no god for lying,
That he has seen Odysseus, that your husband
Is coming home – but it would only tire you.

PENELOPE: It is too late, my friend, the end has come!
But if he wants to ramble I will listen.
I have two halves, a half for hearing stories,
And a hard half for not believing them.

Enter TELEMACHOS.

He comes!

They embrace.

TELEMACHOS: I have to face the suitors now.
But I am glad that you are still alive,
And still unmarried in my father's house.

PENELOPE: This is the last day! He has not come home.
But if he did, their bones would heap these rooms!

TELEMACHOS sneezes. PENELOPE laughs in delight.

See how he sneezes when I speak like that!
Vengeance is pepper! But it will not happen.

TELEMACHOS: Now mother, take your maids and
climb the stairs,
Before the suitors see you here unveiled.

And I will join you in a little while,
To tell you what these eyes of mine have seen.

PENELOPE: Oh I can't wait to hear about the world!

Exit.

TELEMACHOS: Eumaios!

EUMAIOS: Are you mad, Telemachos?
Why have you changed your mind and followed me?
What are you doing in the lion's mouth?

TELEMACHOS: Athene tells me not to be afraid.

EUMAIOS: She is a reckless goddess.

TELEMACHOS: Yes she is.
A reckless goddess is my friend, Eumaios!

EUMAIOS: Dangerous friends, the gods, or so I hear.
What dream has filled you with new hope, young man?
My dreams have been surrounded like a bear
By drooling suitors tearing them to pieces.

TELEMACHOS: What do you mean?

EUMAIOS: Your mother has declared
That she will marry one of them tomorrow.

TELEMACHOS: Trust in Athene.

EUMAIOS: I prefer the Furies.

Enter ANTINOOS.

ANTINOOS: Aha, Telemachos, adventurer!
You have returned! And did you like the mainland?
What did wise Nestor whisper in your ear,
Don't trust that snake Antinoos? Hush, Nestor!
How about Helen? Is she beautiful?
Even more lovely than Penelope?
But not so clever! I would not have sailed

To Troy for her, but for Penelope
I would have burned down any famous city.

TELEMACHOS: In fact they tell me that some friends
of yours

Sailed, at your instigation, recently,
Against a man who loves Penelope,
Antinoos – I think the man was me.
That was a kind of little Trojan war
You fought at one remove. But I am told
That they have just been sighted in the harbour,
These friends of yours, to which they have returned,
Having accomplished absolutely nothing.

ANTINOOS: My son – not yet – male offspring of
the woman

Whose lucky husband I intend to be –
This world is wild, and those who leave their homes,
As men must do, if they are to be known,
Are certain to encounter difficulties,
If not from men or monsters, from the weather,
From the great gods to whom our souls are candles.
And you have faced the chaos and the crisis,
The Trojan war of daily life outside
The warm defences of your mother's chambers.
Come to my arms, young man, a boy no more,
You have stepped laughing from the dragon's mouth,
And I exhalt you, hero, king to be,
Absolute heir of your remembered father.
Sit with the suitors, be our equal now,
Look, we are leaping to the feast again,
Having been dancing down the sinking sun
And hurling lances far into its eye,
This generation racing for one prize!

EUMAIOS: If you are eating then I must be going.

ANTINOOS: No, swineherd, stay, and taste the chops
you raised,
Serious maids are swinging jugs of wine,
And heaping up the tables with good things,
The gods are groaning for our offerings,
And as the sun lays down its head, our men
Prepare the hecatomb to Zeus of cattle
And pigs, the wealth of sacrificed Odysseus;
You shall not turn your back on our rejoicing.

TELEMACHOS: The feast, my friends! But I must
tell my mother
What I have seen.

Exit TELEMACHOS. Enter ODYSSEUS.

ANTINOOS: Oh – dogs must not come in.
Old man, the spiders in your cloak are weaving
Another cloak around it. Kind of them!
You are a crowded house of lice already,
And fleas are drinking your red wine in millions.
But you must entertain them in the yard,
There is not room for two feasts in this house.
Or are you deaf? Then you must smell my breath –
Shoo!
Give me·a broom to brush away this dust,
This cobweb that has caught a human face!

EUMAIOS: Strangers are sacred to the god who thunders.

ANTINOOS: Zeus loves me now. His love for this
has died.

EUMAIOS: The gods hold earth and heaven in
their hands.

ANTINOOS: But I have got his sagging throat in mine!

EUMAIOS: You shall not curse this house! Let go of him!

ANTINOOS: Eumaios, what has made you so unslavelike?

EUMAIOS: He is my guest.

ANTINOOS: The slave invites the beggar!

ANTINOOS throws ODYSSEUS to the ground. EUMAIOS stops ODYSSEUS from leaving.

EUMAIOS: This man is not the master of the house.

ANTINOOS: Now I must kill you. You have crossed the line,
And all my brave companions watching me.

He draws his sword on EUMAIOS. Enter IROS, which distracts ANTINOOS.

Iros, my friend! I shall not go to supper
Unsatisfied!

IROS: Now show me this usurper!

ANTINOOS: We are on Troy plain, Hector and Achilles
Tear through the dust like rival hurricanes –
Oh Illium, the insult to your fame!
This place is this man's patch, the beggar Iros
Believes himself appointed by the gods
Exclusively to scrape for scraps in this,
The palace of invisible Odysseus.
It is a big man, generously fed,
Younger and sleeker than his challenger,
Who is an old bone chewed and chewed again.
Splinter him, Iros – if he stands his ground –
Or will he vanish in a flash? He stands!

ODYSSEUS prepares himself.

And he looks harder than he did before!
Iros retreats! Oh Iros, changed your mind?
I'll cut your balls off!

IROS: I will break your face!

ODYSSEUS: Why are you angry, fellow beggarman?
    Surely the palace of Odysseus
    Is big enough for both of us to stink in?
    You are a big man, but all quivering!
    And I am trim from sparring with Poseidon,
    And mad, from screaming out too many storms!

ANTINOOS: And so Achilles said his piece, and Hector
    Stepped back!

*IROS and ODYSSEUS circle each other, IROS trying to
escape and being pushed back by ANTINOOS.*

                But all along the walls of Troy –
    My friends, forgive me if I call you Trojans –
    The people shouted, have a go at him!
    The gates were barred against retreat, and Hector
    Puffed out his feathers and prepared to perish.
    Hector, that war-cloud, poised his streak of lightning,
    Narrowed his eyes and flung it –

IROS hits ODYSSEUS on the shoulder.

                      but the point
    Bounced off the armoured shoulder of Achilles –
    Mighty Achilles answered him directly –

*ODYSSEUS strikes IROS on the ear and knocks him flat.
IROS sits kicking and crying on the ground.*

Glorious fight! The Trojans on the walls
    Blanched – they had seen their army's head stoved in,
    And in their guts they felt the squirm of doom.
    And swift Achilles stooped and by the heel
    Hauled Hector from the shadow of the wall,
    Still kicking –

ODYSSEUS drags IROS off.

                and he propped him up outside,
    To scare away the dogs and other strays.

Come to my arms, unvanquishable man!
Come sit beside us and rejoice with us!
Eat hard, remind this widow that to marry
One of us, rids her of the rest of us!
The gods would like to join this company;
Tomorrow morning one of us shall seize
The virtue of the earth, Penelope.

ODYSSEUS: Yes, I have heard that she is good to look at.
Could this be her?

*Enter PENELOPE, accompanied by a MAID holding a veil
in front of her face, and by TELEMACHOS.*

ANTINOOS: I cannot speak, my tongue
Has grown too long.

PENELOPE: Telemachos, this house
Has lost its good name. When a stranger comes,
Asking for shelter, as for Zeus we owe him,
And is assaulted in this hall, I hope
That my Odysseus never hears of it,
Or there will be bad days among the living.
But as it is, this stranger, though not young,
Has with his fists beat down a bigger man,
And how I wish that all the feasters here
Could be evicted bleeding from the ears.

ANTINOOS: If all the men in Argos, perfect Queen,
Could see you shining as you do today,
I swear tomorrow they would all be here,
And there would not be room in Ithaka!

PENELOPE: Antinoos, my beauty and my grace
Left me the day my husband left for Troy.
And so I grieve, remembering. He held me
Hard by the wrist, the day he left this house,
And staring straight into my eyes, he said,
'It may not be that I will keep my life

In the close fighting. You must keep this house.
But when you see our sweet son fully grown,
And bearded, you may take another man,
And leave this household.' Now that time has come.
A bitter hateful marriage must be mine,
Because the father of the gods has taken
My happiness away. Since this must be,
Why must you suitors deepen my despair
By not behaving as men used to do,
In giving treasures to the one they wish for?

ANTINOOS: Penelope, you have encouraged us,
Let each man send a herald to his house
To fetch for her the treasures of the earth!
My friends and fellow-suitors, listen to me!
The sight of her for whom we fight through life,
First makes me silent like a hiding bird,
Then builds up words like summer storms inside,
That have to let down rain. Oh hear my passion
For this moon-woman. Did the gods above us
Become immortal at the touch of beauty
Like this above them? Oh my hopeful friends,
We are like worms, or worse than worms, the ground,
Given one hope in its oblivion,
The passing pressure of this windblown woman.

PENELOPE: Antinoos, I thank you for your grace.

Exit PENELOPE and MAID.

ANTINOOS: And she is gone, and I am just a man,
And now a worm, and now the littered ground.
Each man who sits and feasts beneath her knows
That she could make him finer with her eyes
Than he was ever born to be! Your bones
Would spring again if she believed in you,
Old beggar, you are groaning in your soul,
To have the glimmer of a chance like mine!

But you can still enjoy yourself with us!
You are the heir of Iros. But take care,
I am a strange man, capable of change.
Be patient and endure me, if you can,
Otherwise vanish. I must be myself.
Swineherd! My friend! The only honest man!

*Exit ANTINOOS. EUMAIOS avoids him and exits. Only
TELEMACHOS and ODYSSEUS remain.*

ODYSSEUS: To make a profit from a pack of hounds
Even as they are tearing you to pieces!
That was a dance-step worthy of Odysseus!
It is like victory to look at her.
But we will lose her if we let that show.

TELEMACHOS: Father, the walls are leaping suddenly
As if a fire was blazing in the corner.

ODYSSEUS: It is Athene saying – no delay!
We must remove the weapons from the walls,
And hide them where the suitors will not find them
When they most need them. So we build their pyre.

Enter EURYKLEIA.

EURYKLEIA: The Queen my mistress wants to see
                                            the stranger,
To hear the news he brings about Odysseus.

ODYSSEUS: (*To TELEMACHOS.*)
Do it alone. Athene will be with you.
And tell Eumaios not to leave the palace.

Exeunt.

Scene 6

PENELOPE in an upstairs chamber, singing, accompanied by a lyre.

PENELOPE: Agamemnon and Cassandra
Lying in the ship together

On the way from windy Troy.
Long the journey, brief their joy.

Clytaemnestra and Aegistheus
Kiss in Agamemnon's palace –
Oh the infamy of life,
She is Agamemnon's wife.

Agamemnon at his table
Eats as much as he is able;
Suddenly a web descends
On the husband and his friends.

And Aegistheus swings the axe,
Agamemnon's bones it cracks,
And the Furies lift their heads,
Sniff the wind and leave their beds –

Enter ODYSSEUS led by EURYKLEIA.

EURYKLEIA: Queen, I have brought the man you want
to see.

Wring him out roughly, I advise, my lady,
He can speak well, but something suddenly
Catches his eye, and he curls up and dies.
But if you glimpse the circles of his mind,
And pick them out like medals from a bag,
You will have asked the swallow what it knows
About the lanes and turnings of the air.

Exit.

PENELOPE: Dear Eurykleia, thank you. Welcome, sir!
Sit down, if you are able, by the fire;
I think you are a man who likes to stand,
Those feet are braced against a deck that yaws
Away from waves. As for myself, I long
To sweep about, and stagger here and there.

ODYSSEUS: Lady, no man on earth could find in you
Anything to condemn. Your reputation

Rises to heaven, like the sacred name
Of some great king who rules with such discretion
That the black earth holds nothing back from him.

ATHENE: (*Aside.*)
From courtesies and niceties
Like a caged bird the wild heart cries.
Oh how can these unbordered birds,
The geese of love, be caged in words?

PENELOPE: I lack the conversation of my husband.
That is my problem. Do you understand?
All other men are enemies, their praise
Roughens my skin. But you, it seems to me,
Are, in a small way, something like that man.
Tomorrow is the day when he and I
Must part forever, even in the mind.

CHORUS: So speak to her as if you were
Odysseus – if he still exists!

PENELOPE: We two were equals. When I threw a stone,
It turned into a swallow in his mind,
If that was what I wanted – or the wound
Would open wide and turn into a chasm
That he would lift me out of. So we swayed,
Until that woman carried him away –
Helen, I mean, who stole from many women
Their rightful husbands, like a charming grave.

ODYSSEUS: I fought for her, and it is hard for me
To speak against her.

PENELOPE: 			In the shadows there,
Where you like standing, you could be my husband.
Oh step into the light and speak your mind
Before I fall in love with you, my friend.
That would be too hospitable of me.
But here, you see, all rules of right behaviour

Have drifted to the brink, and some gone over,
Our culture creaks, and is about to shatter
Like a weak bucket full of stormy water.
I hold the old ways by this thread – my posture,
And my back aches, believe me. Yes, like water
I will go down at last into the gutter.

ATHENE: (*Aside.*)
Hold back the sea, you must be dammed
And trickle through a sluicegate gently.

ODYSSEUS: These men are ruthless, worthless and unjust,
You are a woman on your own among them;
The whole world sings about the way you hold them,
And hopes that soon your husband will return,
Which you have earned. And I have news of him.

PENELOPE: Of that you must convince me, be my guide
Back to the land of hope whose coasts are golden;
At present I am wandering insane
In a dark land, where everything is dying;
But you appeared, a man without pretensions,
Bearing the honesty of rags, a king
In that you would not let them put you down;
And the commotion reached me in my room,
So that I almost thought that man had come;
So I am pouring foolishness upon you,
Because this is my last night with my husband.
Noble old man, despite your present fortune,
Where have you come from? In my mind I see you
Raised in some unimaginable kingdom
Where justice is the child of heroism.

CHORUS: Now a sea whispers to a sea
And just a streak of land between.

ODYSSEUS: Oh do not ask where I have been, my lady.
To cry a river in another man's

Palace, and in your sight, would not be fitting.
You have a grief at least as great as mine,
And you are dry-eyed. If I start to cry,
You will despise me, or yourself dissolve,
And should we two sit weeping in this place,
Rather than try to make each other bright?
Let sea-mist wrap what I have done and seen.

PENELOPE: No – we should cry! For twenty years
my bones
Have carried absence – I have raised my son
Without his father setting eyes on him –
A man I love! And I have never known
If I would ever see that face again –
And I have searched for love in leaves and stones
And in my son's eyes, deep into my dreams,
But it is not there, it is lost with him
On the cold ocean or on some wild island.
But I have not changed – and I see that faith
Also in you. The gods have kicked you down,
But you have clung to something, kept your name,
Not like these suitors who have come to nothing!

ODYSSEUS: My name is Aithon, and my father was
Deukalion, the son of Minos, King
Of Crete which is the place where I was born.
I saw Odysseus on his way to Troy.
He stopped to pay a visit to my brother
Idomeneus.

PENELOPE: Stories, places, names!
You I believe, but you must give me signs.
What was my husband wearing?

ODYSSEUS: He was clothed
In a thick purple mantle made of wool;
It had a double fold, and it was held

Together by a golden pin, adorned
With double sheaths, and at the front, a fawn
Caught in the strangling forepaws of a hound.
And under that, the tunic he was in –
It was as smooth and shining as the dried
Skin of an onion; crowds of girls and women
Stood gazing at it – always with your husband
Was a dark man, round-shouldered, woolly-haired,
Eurybates his herald, whom he prized.

CHORUS: Strength of the dead bring down Odysseus!

PENELOPE: (*Weeping.*) The mantle and the tunic
                                              you describe,

   I folded them myself, the day he climbed
   Into the black ship, never to return.

ODYSSEUS: Weeping is easy, and it does you good;
   But you must keep a store of tears for joy
   At his return.

PENELOPE: When will that be? Where is he?

ATHENE: (*Aside.*)
   What is a boat? A well-made lie
   In which a man can cross the sea,
   Which is itself a compromise
   Of rivers and a changing story.

ODYSSEUS: My life has shown me many coasts
                                              and countries

   In my long journey out of grace, my lady.
   And I was in the kingdom of Thesprotia
   Before unjust men brought me to your kingdom.
   And there King Pheidon told me that your husband
   Had sheltered in his house not long before.
   Odysseus could have sailed to Ithaka
   At any time, but he was travelling,
   Collecting wealth from princes who received him,

Because Odysseus is a friend to many.
Finally he had journeyed to Dodona,
To ask the oak about his homecoming,
Whether he should return like Agamemnon
Openly, after such a time, or hidden.

PENELOPE: Old man, I know you speak the truth,
                                             your signs
Were certain, and there is no falseness in you.
But what you say has come too late to save me.

ODYSSEUS: I swear on my good name –

PENELOPE: I had a dream.
I saw my geese, the flock I love and feed,
Snatched by an eagle suddenly and killed,
And a cascade of bloody feathers fell.
And in the morning when I woke I opened
The window, saw them well and cried for joy.

ODYSSEUS: The eagle is Odysseus and the geese
The suitors he will pluck with bloody claws.

PENELOPE: But if my future is Antinoos,
I am the feathers falling out of heaven;
I cannot weave another day of waiting.
Odysseus, come! But if you do not come,
Then I must find the man most like my man.
Odysseus, husband, come into my mind,
Whatever sea or death-cave you are in,
Our minds are still one. Fill me with your wisdom,
And show me how to make the best of things.

ODYSSEUS: Set them a test.

PENELOPE: I know – of course – his bow.
Only a man with arms like his could bend
That stubborn weapon. And he used to set
A row of axe-heads in the ground and shoot

Through all their sockets, touching none of them.
Whichever of the suitors can perform
This feat, at least he has my husband's arms.

ODYSSEUS: The man who bends the bow will be
your husband,
He will return before tomorrow morning.
I swear as sure as I am standing here,
That everything is well, and will be better.

PENELOPE: Old storyteller in the night, old father
Telling brave tales to comfort your grandaughter –
Bless you! Your eyes are brighter than the stars;
But the true past gets buried in the present,
Which is all lies. My fear remains unshaken.
My eyes are closing! But this test tomorrow,
We will enjoy that! Take him to a bed,
Dear Eurykleia, and I hope that dreams
Hold us both fast in what we wish for most
Until the light comes.

Enter EURYKLEIA.

ODYSSEUS: And the light will come.

CHORUS: How sweet, tonight, to be a figment,
But in the morning you must change
Into yourself, and suffer judgement.

Exeunt.

Scene 7

EUMAIOS and TELEMACHOS on the porch.

TELEMACHOS: Eumaios, stay, do not desert the palace,
I would not like to die tonight.

EUMAIOS: Nor me,
Not in this place. What makes you stay? Athene?

TELEMACHOS: No one can harm the man whose
                                    cause she favours.

EUMAIOS: And who might that be?

TELEMACHOS: She has changed the world.

EUMAIOS: Well I am utterly confused, quite frankly,
    But I am with you. I will not abandon
    The son of him we mourn. I will lie down
    Under the courtyard oak and watch you sleeping
    Here on the porch. The stars are my distraction
    From all the shit that happens under heaven.

Exit EUMAIOS. Enter ODYSSEUS and EURYKLEIA.

EURYKLEIA: Sleep here, old fellow. Oh, Telemachos!

TELEMACHOS: I am not sleeping in my room tonight.

EURYKLEIA: You might decide you rather like your room
    When he starts talking – he wore out your mother.

TELEMACHOS: He has come far. Sleep well,
                                    dear Eurykleia.

EURYKLEIA: Sleep well. Tomorrow we will lose
                                    your mother.

Exit EURYKLEIA.

ODYSSEUS: And now the night is full of signs –
    Not still – the stars are teeth that glitter
    Behind swift-moving lips that mutter
    Quick incantations, under eyes
    That are all dark and inward-drowned.
    Athene, do not let us die!

TELEMACHOS: Our cause
    Is hers – or else she would have let you drown.

ODYSSEUS: When she is here, my heart is full of her,
    But when she leaves me I am just Odysseus.

TELEMACHOS: But you don't doubt her.

ODYSSEUS: Doubt is what I am.

TELEMACHOS: A man can trust the promise of
a goddess.

ODYSSEUS: Her purpose is beyond our understanding.

TELEMACHOS: The trap is set, the animals are in it.

ODYSSEUS: But are the hunters us or them? The end
Alone explains the omens. This I know;
Tomorrow I shall speak my name again.

CHORUS: Odysseus, look, the cave is closed,
And in the morning you will die!

ODYSSEUS: There is a story you should know.
We were imprisoned in a cave
By a great evil with one eye.
I told the giant that my name
Was No one, and we sank a spike
Into his eye when he was sleeping,
And the blood bubbled on his face,
And he woke blind and screaming, crying
Help me! – his neighbours at the door,
Which was a giant loaf of stone
Wedged in the cavemouth, called aloud,
'Who has attacked you in the night,
Tell us his name and we will kill him.'
And the blind giant bellowed, 'No one,
No one has stabbed me in the eye,
And I am blind and it was No one.'
And they all shouted back, 'If No one
Has hurt you, but your eye has gone,
It must have been the gods who did it,
And over them we have no power.'

TELEMACHOS laughs.

47

But I would like to tell my wife my name,
And hear her say it, after all this time,
And I would like Telemachos to be
A name less secret than Odysseus.

TELEMACHOS: A name as famous as Achilles!

ODYSSEUS: I saw Achilles, glory of the world,
Burned on a big pyre, watched his grey smoke age
The moon, that maiden, and I turned to stare
At Troy unsightly as the sun fell speared.
Soldier Achilles, when you were alive
You were as honoured as a god. No man
Has ever been more blessed; and even there,
Among the moon-eyed dead your name is honoured.
(*To CHORUS.*) You are Achilles!

CHORUS: I am not that man.

ODYSSEUS: Who are you then? Why do you follow me?

TELEMACHOS: Who are you speaking to?

ODYSSEUS: A man called No one.

TELEMACHOS: Are you afraid?

ODYSSEUS: There is no ground beneath me.

TELEMACHOS: You are a man who fought with
Agamemnon!

ODYSSEUS: If I had cried to him at Troy, 'Come quickly,
I am outnumbered,' he would not have left me
To fight alone. But now his arms are air.
Tomorrow I must face a hundred spears
With just my son beside me, if Athene –
Black silence, nothing stirring in the army.
We should have left that woman with the Trojans!

TELEMACHOS: Odysseus!

ODYSSEUS: I have drunk a sea of poison,
And now my cup is full again! I struggled
With all my mind, to bring down Illium,
And then it fell, and burned, and in the burning,
I looked around, for all my great companions
To share the crown – and something caught my eye,
Far down the smoky alley of the sky –
And it was them, Achilles and Patroklos
And all the rest, but they were dogs, that shivered.
That was a chasm. Sitting by the shore
For seven years, imprisoned by Calypso,
I tried to fill it with my tears, but only
Saw worse disasters in the depths reflected,
And the whole curse is gathered in this moment,
No part of it is absent from my spirit,
But every death, and every storm, remembered,
Crowds inward, wide-eyed, and my safety dwindles.
And all I say is this: have mercy on me,
Athene! Touch me with some certainty!
Speak to me, dead man, drink my blood, and help me!

He cuts himself. Enter EUMAIOS.

EUMAIOS: What is this shouting? Are you being
                                    murdered?

TELEMACHOS: Eumaios, this old man is full
                                    of nightmares,
But I will get him back to sleep, don't worry.

EUMAIOS: This is a bad night.

TELEMACHOS: Not a night for resting.

EUMAIOS: There is no wind but we are in a storm.

Exit EUMAIOS.

CHORUS: Listen, Odysseus, I am not
One person, I am your companions,

All those who perished in the sea,
And we drift stinking on the green,
And we beach, nameless, on dead shores,
And crabs applaud us with their claws.

ODYSSEUS: Why do you turn against me? It was me
Thought of the horse, and packed in my companions,
Climbed in behind them. And I saw the plain
Dragged with the lines of silent women slaves,
Like ants that carry sugar from a pantry,
But slower. How the ground was packed with husbands
Beneath their feet, and how the gods were glutted,
Death glutted, sleepy, hate a moment happy!
To find my way, I delve into my mind,
As once I dug into the sunless ground
Of the Kimmerians and raised up phantoms!
What is your case against me? I have heard
The sirens singing, and I am alive –
Is that my crime? I broke the spell of Circe.
Set free her swine – I hung above the whirlpool
Under the monsters' cave – I saw the seabed
Open and close – I smelt the sun god's cattle
Roasting, felt death's noose closing, saw the end
Rising in fury from an untied bag.
I am the man who saw and did these things.
See how they hurry to the blood like hounds!

CHORUS: Odysseus, listen to my wisdom.
I have a prophecy for you;
When you come home, and you have cleansed
Your palace of its filth and scum,
You must begin another journey,
Further than all your former travels.
Sail to the mainland. With your oar
Upon your shoulder, walk inland
Far from the homes of sailing men.
And this will be a certain sign:
When a man takes the oar you carry

For a new kind of winnowing fan,
Then you will know that you have left
All knowledge of the sea behind.
Set your oar upright in the ground
And sacrifice to great Poseidon
One ram, one bull, one boar. Return
To your established palace then.

ODYSSEUS: How will I die?

CHORUS: In old age, peacefully.
But we will wander in the air
As chaff, or starlings in a storm!
So all earth's mountains shall be broken,
Rock fall on rock, her shining mansions
Collapse, all gold, all good be scattered!

ODYSSEUS: Furies, tear Helen, make her ugly!

TELEMACHOS: Father, consider: if we die tomorrow,
Think of the great companions we will join
And how at last all agony will end
As we descend together, hand in hand.

ODYSSEUS collapses. TELEMACHOS puts a blanket over him. ODYSSEUS sleeps.

Enter EUMAIOS.

EUMAIOS: Alright?

TELEMACHOS: Alright.

EUMAIOS: I think the stars are fading.

Exit EUMAIOS.

CHORUS: Now sleep, a moment, as the light
Begins its wide advance, in silence.
The glaring stars retreat reluctant

By twos and threes from the attack
Of the bold sun, the hero-king,
Who will go down after much fighting.

Exeunt.

Scene 8

Dawn. Enter ANTINOOS testing the bow, not using his full strength.

ANTINOOS: Now be as supple as the wit and wiles
    Of beautiful Antinoos, although
    You are the will of stiff Penelope.
    Athene, breaker of battalions, hear me,
    And open out my little crying life
    To the horizons of Penelope!
    Now come, companions, to our morning feast,
    And when our blood is strengthened with the wine
    Of lost Odysseus, we must win his wife.

Enter EUMAIOS.

Swineherd, my brother! Here you are again,
I thought you would have left us in the night,
But you are here! Increase the celebration,
Life is worth living!

Enter TELEMACHOS.

               And the handsome son,
Ready to give his mother to the winner,
And to be master of his father's house!
Whoever wins her gives you victory!

Enter ODYSSEUS.

And my heart drops from heaven to the ground,
Like a shot bird. The prince precedes the beggar.
I have accepted that you knocked out Iros,
And how could I receive my rightful prize,

If I denied you yours? But watch yourself,
I do not like your face, I don't know why.

ODYSSEUS: Antinoos, forgive me for my face.
Consider that I was a man of power.
Pity me now, all fenced around with fears
That keep the wild beasts in, not out; alone,
With no one on this earth to fight for me.

He holds out his wallet to ANTINOOS for alms.

ANTINOOS: Then go to Hades and employ the Furies!

*ANTINOOS roars and flings an ox-hoof which misses
ODYSSEUS.*

Oh for a son to rid me of this weasel!
But nobody obeys me in this palace.
Give me red wine, and I will change the future!

ODYSSEUS: (*To TELEMACHOS, aside.*)
Order the maid to lock the outer doors.

Exit TELEMACHOS. EUMAIOS and ODYSSEUS talk aside.

EUMAIOS: I am convinced that we have reached the time
When misery has settled on the world:
Not tragedy, the tragedy has happened;
And there will be no change of any kind
Except from fear to horror to despair
And back to terror on the sad-go-round.
Only the old and utterly insane
Still talk about their happy dreams, in rhyme.

ODYSSEUS: I am Odysseus.

EUMAIOS: I am Aphrodite.

ODYSSEUS: What would convince you?

EUMAIOS: Nothing you could say!

ODYSSEUS: If I had known that at my homecoming
　　There would be groans, I would have gladly drowned.
　　Eumaios! I beseech you, sad old man,
　　Have one last spasm of imagination;
　　We used to laugh until we dribbled, friend!
　　I need you now!

EUMAIOS:　　　Too many things are true.

ODYSSEUS: Which will you choose?

EUMAIOS:　　　　　　He used to have a scar
　　Up his right thigh, a bad one, from a boar
　　When he was young. If you can show me that,
　　That would be proof. I reckon no two men
　　Could have that stretched-out crescent. Lift your rags,
　　And if there's nothing, everything's the same,
　　But if the scar's there, heaven help these suitors.

　　ODYSSEUS shows him the scar.

　　Zeus.

ODYSSEUS:　Now Eumaios, keep it to yourself!
　　And fight beside me when I shoot the bow!

EUMAIOS: Zeus.

　　Enter PENELOPE, veiled.

PENELOPE:　　Now begin the contest of the bow!

　　Re-enter TELEMACHOS.

ANTINOOS: Stand up! You suitors, do not fear this trial,
　　Now you must win, your destiny is waiting,
　　Invisible, to be revealed, its veil
　　Torn open and its lands of plenty taken!
　　If she is wise, if she is beautiful,
　　You should be able to pull down the sky.
　　We have missed Helen. We did not see Troy;
　　But we are happy with Penelope.

ODYSSEUS

Achilles was a comet in his rage,
And Hector's death was like the moon, they say;
Our war is smaller, but our love is greater,
Vaster than any that took fire at Troy.
So let us lift our own lives up, and praise
Our struggle with each other for this lady,
Whose husband nothing weaker than the sea
Could have restrained from her defence this day!

TELEMACHOS: I shall try first, and hope to keep
                                    my mother.

ANTINOOS: Telemachos!

*TELEMACHOS tries the bow and almost bends it.
ODYSSEUS signals him not to.*

TELEMACHOS: But my youth fails me. I am not yet sure
    Of what my hands can do, and so I falter.

ANTINOOS: Give me the bow. My love is like the sun
    That draws out hosts of gold from seeds that dream,
    And lifts the earth from winter with no hands.

TELEMACHOS: Antinoos!

ANTINOOS tries the bow and fails to string it.

ANTINOOS: At the first try my love has died away,
    But it grows stronger at the sight of her!

He tries and fails again.

Perhaps the lady is not beautiful –

He tries again and fails.

It is this day! This is a holiday,
A holy feast day. How can we be strong
When no one else is working? It would be
Impossible to fight on such a day,
Never mind bend the spirit in this thing.
Penelope cannot be won today,

55

And we should join the celebrations! Friends,
No one but I will fail this test today –
You must not try it – do we all agree?

ODYSSEUS: Forgive me, masters, may I try the weapon?

ANTINOOS: What was that noise? A kind of groan –
                                          a dog
  Trying to roar.

ODYSSEUS: I beat the beggarman.

ANTINOOS: And will you marry sweet Penelope?
  Old fellow, she can smell and she can see –

ODYSSEUS: No sir, I only want to try my hands.
  This is good sport, and you can laugh at me
  Failing to bend this thing, or be spurred on
  If even I can do it.

ANTINOOS: Man of grime,
  This is a trial of love, and not a game;
  I warned you once that I am prone to change,
  And I will take you by the throat again!

PENELOPE: Shameful! To think that those who fight
                                  for me
  Should fear a rival older than their fathers!

TELEMACHOS: Mother, go up, and sit beside your loom,
  And think about Odysseus as you bend
  To the unending work of women. Men
  Possess this hall, and I above all others
  Control this bow, and say whose hands it goes to.

PENELOPE: This is a man, my child has not returned.

Exit PENELOPE. EUMAIOS takes the bow to ODYSSEUS.

ANTINOOS: What are you doing, swineherd? Put
                                    that down!

TELEMACHOS: Eumaios, you may take it to the stranger.
   If this man stops you, I will throw him out!

ANTINOOS: Son of a hero!

He laughs.

ODYSSEUS: If my hands retain
   The power of my youth despite the tides,
   This bow will not resist me. See, it yields.
   This is how much I love Penelope.

He shoots the arrow.

ANTINOOS: Straight through the hoops!
   Ah, Penelope,
   This victory has made you ugly! Hades!
   Beggarman! Death! Odysseus!

*ODYSSEUS catches him again. He strangles ANTINOOS
to death.*

ODYSSEUS: Troy is burning in the moonlight!

TELEMACHOS: Where is Athene?

Enter ATHENE.

ATHENE: I am here!

ODYSSEUS: Ah goddess!

ATHENE: Did you fear?

ODYSSEUS: (*Shouts as a war cry.*)
   Achilles!

Exeunt.

Scene 9

PENELOPE asleep in her chamber. Enter ATHENE.

ATHENE: I dance on time, I dance for him,
   I dance creation and destruction;

Almost a god, and yet not proud,
This is my work, a man, my darling,
So now I tear you out of me;
She has deserved you with her cunning;
And blood is running in your rooms
To prove the value of devotion,
And all the pressure of the ocean
Will rush from him to you, providing
The sacrifice to me most fitting.

She wakes PENELOPE, and exits.

PENELOPE: Odysseus? Nothing!

Enter TELEMACHOS covered in blood.

TELEMACHOS: Mother!

PENELOPE: Odysseus!

TELEMACHOS: He is in the house,
And we have killed the suitors.

PENELOPE: All of them?

TELEMACHOS: You should have seen your husband,
           like a storm,
His hands and forearms red, his face the same;
I can still see him clearer than this room;
Oh now I know the fighting does not end
When all your enemies are dead.

PENELOPE: My son,
Listen to me. So you have fought a battle.
And who was with you?

TELEMACHOS: Merciless Eumaios
The swineherd, great Athene, and Odysseus.
And he has freed Eumaios and has promised
To give him not just freedom but a house
Close to his own, and sheepflocks and a wife,

And hold him dearly as his close companion
Until the day he dies – Eumaios dances
And sings in praise of his sad life, because
Beyond his years of slavery and pigs
The day was waiting when he would be thanked!

PENELOPE: And you are certain that this is Odysseus?

TELEMACHOS: The man is coming to you now.
His years

Of absence have been cut down in their prime –
At nineteen, bright, at twenty dead and gone!

PENELOPE: Is he still shaking with the battle rage?

TELEMACHOS: His nurse has washed him. You will
recognise him.

It is Odysseus!

PENELOPE: One would almost think
That you had seen him. But we must remember
The playful gods, and our own wishful thinking.

TELEMACHOS: He will be coming. I must not be here.
I have believed him, never having seen him;
Your memory and love could not deceive you.

Exit TELEMACHOS.

PENELOPE: And if it is Odysseus, who is that,
After so long? And what am I to him?
Athene, save me, make the man who comes
Equal to the Odysseus in my mind!

Enter ODYSSEUS.

ODYSSEUS: Lady, I have returned again. The man
Who said last night that I would come, has come.

PENELOPE: My friend. I did not recognise you then,
And so I do not recognise you now.

ODYSSEUS: That is extremely strange.

PENELOPE: I clearly see
    Odysseus as he stepped into his ship
    With his companions twenty years ago,
    But if you are my husband, you have changed.

ODYSSEUS: You are the strictest woman in the world.
    And like a man who, having clung all day
    To a thin branch above a roaring lion,
    At last let down, he can't ungrip his hands –
    Your mind is clinging to the old illusion
    That I am gone, that you are still in danger.

PENELOPE: Anyone can be urgent. And the world
    Is full of men who look like other men.
    And if another man, a shadow-man
    Came to persuade me, he would speak like you.

ODYSSEUS: Dear lady, there is cause for urgency;
    But I can match you if you wish, and stay
    At arm's length, till Athene clears your eyes.
    Now I am weary. I have cleansed your house;
    I need to sleep – perhaps your nurse could make me
    A bed downstairs, and I will try again
    To be Odysseus to your satisfaction
    Tomorrow.

PENELOPE: I shall make you this concession –
    That she will take your own bed out – I mean
    His bed, and set it up for you to sleep on
    Downstairs. And I will pray to great Athene
    To teach my mind the truth of this.

ODYSSEUS: Strange lady,
    What are you saying? Have you lost your mind?
    I built our bed around an olive tree,
    This is a thing that no one else has seen,
    The trunk supports it and is part of it.

Has someone cut the olive at the root
And with four horses carted off my bed?

PENELOPE: Odysseus!

ODYSSEUS: So often in the past it would have been
Death to have heard my name. When I was spying
In Troy and Helen recognised me, and
When I was hiding in the giant's cave.
Now it is life. And so I cast off No one,
And watch him sink into the deepening
Of the sea's eye. And now I stand unguarded.
Loved, and exposed, as you remember me.
I must forget the tricks of hate, and learn
To be Odysseus where that man is known.
Say it again – strip off another skin.

PENELOPE: Odysseus!

ODYSSEUS: Penelope.

PENELOPE: No other voice on earth can say
                               that name

In such a way that it means anything.
They say it, but they cannot make it sound
Like anything but what they want from me.

ODYSSEUS: And I must make another journey –

PENELOPE: Where?

ODYSSEUS: Sail to the mainland – with your oar
Upon your shoulder, walk inland
Far from the homes of sailing men.
And this will be a certain sign:
When someone takes the oar you carry
For a new kind of winnowing fan,
Set your oar upright in the ground,
And sacrifice to great Poseidon

One ram, one bull, one boar – return
To your established palace then.

PENELOPE: It is not finished.

ODYSSEUS: I have come back home,
But still the thunder of the sea invades me,
The crust above the underworld we walk on
For me is broken, and the dead surround me.
One thing is finished. You have kept yourself
Free from the fate of Helen and the wife
Of Agamemnon. You and I are one,
Those two can take the burden of disaster,
Carry Achilles on their slender shoulders,
While you preserve the honour of Odysseus
Next to your name, and all the praise for patience.

PENELOPE: Husband, explain things patiently to me.

ODYSSEUS: No need for patience when I speak to you.

PENELOPE: They say Calypso in Ogygia
Offered Odysseus immortality.
Why did he not accept it?

ODYSSEUS: He was tired.

PENELOPE: Of what?

ODYSSEUS: Of pebbles.

PENELOPE: And they say that Circe
Bewitched Odysseus when she had transformed
His grunting friends into themselves again.
Did he desire her, or was his desire
For the way home she knew?

ODYSSEUS: She knew the door
To Hades. And the prophet rose from there,
Who knew the way home. Also many others,

Who must be put back. I have said my name,
And it is in the open, like a ring;
Now I return into the sea of eyes
That never close, to lead home my companions,
Who have upheld me with their death, returned
To you, Odysseus. When I come again
There will be no more taking to the waves,
And you and I will speak for years and days
About the speaking monsters we have seen;
I have to tell you how my men devoured
The cattle of the sun god and were drowned;
How the wind pushed us almost to our home,
When Aeolus had knotted in a bag
The weather; which my men let loose, for gold,
Blowing us back beyond our first horizon;
I have to tell you what the Sirens sing;
And Scylla pushing men into her mouths,
Must be described; and when you have received
The height and depth, I will be well again,
But that is not yet.

PENELOPE: Which of all the gods,
Jealous that our two minds are one, decided
To stop us from becoming one another
At ease at home? But love of you preserved
My strength when you were nowhere in the world,
And I have not changed. Now the old wind rises,
And it may not return you. But this waiting
Has made me wider than the world, you sail
Towards me when you sail away from me,
You will be sailing on my patience, even
In Hades you could not escape from me,
And I will end in you and you in me.

They embrace and exeunt different ways.

CHORUS: Now Orestes with his sword
Cuts his mother from the world,

63

Shudders in the cringing hills;
Helen in her palace cries
As Achilles in her dreams
Asks her for his generation;
And Odysseus feels the world
Give beneath a keel again;
But Penelope alone
On her island with her son
Folds them all in one horizon
And her patience is the end.

The End.